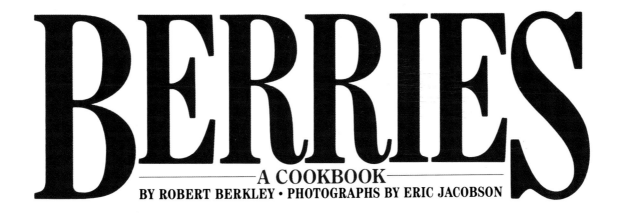

BERRIES

A COOKBOOK

BY ROBERT BERKLEY · PHOTOGRAPHS BY ERIC JACOBSON

DESIGN BY LESLEY EHLERS

A FIRESIDE BOOK

PUBLISHED BY SIMON & SCHUSTER INC.

NEW YORK   LONDON   TORONTO   SYDNEY   TOKYO

A RUNNING HEADS BOOK

 Fireside
Simon & Schuster Building
Rockefeller Center
1230 Avenue of the Americas
New York, New York 10020

BERRIES: A COOKBOOK
was produced and conceived by
Running Heads Incorporated
55 West 21st Street
New York, New York 10010

Senior Editor: Sarah Kirshner
Production Manager: Linda Winters
Managing Editor: Lindsey Crittenden

10   9   8   7   6   5   4   3   2

Library of Congress Cataloging in Publication Data

Berkley, Robert.
    Berries : a cookbook / Robert Berkley ; Photographs by Eric
Jacobson.
        p.   cm.
    "A Fireside book."
    ISBN 0-671-69019-1
    1. Cookery (Berries)   I. Title.
TX813.B4B47   1990
641.6'47—dc20   89-19675
                                                          CIP

Typeset by Trufont Typographers, Inc.
Color Separations by Hong Kong Scanner Craft Company, Ltd.
Printed and bound in Singapore by Times Offset Pte Ltd.

To my mother, my grandparents and Michelle.

Special thanks to Mary Trasko, Mildred Raucher and Mary Forsell for
their contributions of materials for this book. Thanks to Michelle Hauser,
Nancy and Sam Freitag, Loretta and Bruno Hauser, Kate Struby, Meggin
Siefert, Robin Page, Maggie Jones, Judy Devine, Myriam Zwierzinska,
Doug Hay, Rick Silverness, Jennifer Barnaby, prop stylist, and Brendan
Mullany, photo assistant. Thanks to Marta Hallett, Ellen Milionis, Sarah
Kirshner, Lindsey Crittenden and all the other support at Running Heads,
and to Caroline Herter and Rebecca Verrill at Simon & Schuster.

Thanks to the following for their generosity: ABC Bed Bath and Linens;
Marek Cecula, designer, and Pascal Golay, designer; Contemporary
Porcelain; Gear Stores; Bill Goldsmith, plate designer; Marble Connection;
Umbrello.

CONTENTS

CHAPTER FOUR
DESSERTS

CHAPTER FIVE
BEVERAGES

INTRODUCTION

When I think of berries, the first thing that comes to mind is a sensation I experienced as a teenager. I was driving through central North Carolina with a friend on a sunny late morning in June. We were driving on a state highway when we found ourselves along a series of mountains, and decided to stop the car by the base of one of the mountains to hike.

Since there were no paths through the thickets, we had to create one. After a long climb we rested, and while catching our breath from the heat and the strenuous hike, we noticed a blackberry bush. We each dared the other to try a berry; one of us finally did, and when he didn't keel over from poison, and found that it was good, we managed to devour almost every berry on that bush.

Every time I eat a really fresh berry, I recall the combination of the sun, the fresh air, the mountains of North Carolina, being sixteen and the supreme sensual experience of the slightly sour berry juice bursting between my teeth. Even the word "berries" is enough to evoke the abundance of all these sensations.

It took me a long time and certain prejudices to overcome before I began cooking with berries; I didn't want to spoil their organic intensity. After all, cooking is by definition a process of destruction: breaking down fibers, altering flavors, changing forms. How could a fresh berry be improved? Cooking with berries demands different expectations and requires a different approach. Within each berry lies a multitude of different flavors and textures which can be drawn out to do whatever you as a cook want them to do. Depending on the demands of a dish, the elements within a berry can be used to thicken sauce, change color, balance spiciness, counteract bitterness—all while lending to the dish the distinct and sublime character of the particular berry. The idea of drawing out more savory and fuller, rounder flavors from a berry can be a very exciting challenge to an inquisitive cook.

The recipes in this book are designed to illustrate the diversity of cooking with berries. In some cases simply adding a fresh berry to an assortment of ingredients is all that is required, the pristine state of the berry speaking for itself within the arrangement of the dish. In other cases we put the berry through various cooking stages to elicit the different degrees of character in each berry. In fact almost entire identities change in different cooking processes.

For example, in comparing Blueberry Vichyssoise with Blueberry Pie, it's hard to believe the same ingredient is used in both dishes. The different tastes of the same berry in reaction to the other ingredients—one earthy, potatoey, the other syrupy, fruity and sweet—demonstrates two parts of the spectrum of this wide-ranging fruit.

Another striking example is what can happen to a soup when we substitute berries for other ingredients. Gazpacho calls for tartness. Usually a little vinegar or lemon juice fills that vacancy and gently supports the other ingredients—tomato, cucumbers, peppers—so that the focus of attention is on them, while the lemon or vinegar acts as a sort of post, quietly holding up the structure. In Cranberry Gazpacho, the cranberry is gentle enough not to overshadow everything else but intense enough to be the dominant flavor of the soup, with the other ingredients acting in support of it—an exciting variation on a traditional dish.

In a similar vein, I have chosen closely related recipes that share certain procedures and ingredients but use different berries. In Smoked Trout and Raspberry Salad with Lingonberry Dressing, raspberries are used for their soft flavor. A more sour berry would certainly work well with the bitter flavor of the arugula, but would confound the saltiness of the smoked fish. In the Bitter Greens Salad with Strawberries and Gooseberry Vinaigrette, strawberries are used so as not to detract from the sharpness of the goat cheese. The common element in both salads is the bitter flavor of the greens. Both berries work comfortably with their other accompaniments—the smoked trout and the cheese—and these accompaniments work equally well with the greens. What becomes interesting is the flavors that become apparent in the *greens* when combined with the *berries*. The bitterness seems to change when introduced to the exceptionally subtle differences in the two berries. The recipes illustrate the range of character of each berry and its capacity to work well with other ingredients in a way that a straight taste test between a strawberry and a raspberry could not.

The fragility of flavor that makes berries so desirable isn't always easy to obtain. You can't always be on a Carolina mountainside when blackberries reach their height of perfection. As with many other types of produce, different berries are in season at different times and do not grow for much of the rest of the year, nor do they grow in the most accessible places. Blueberries are in season in the Northern Atlantic States from August through September, and are in season in New Zealand through March to early April. Cranberries are in season in North America from early November through mid-February. Strawberries are in season in mid-June to July, raspberries are available May through June, but many berries are now available year-round. It is rare to experience a really fresh cloudberry at any time outside Scandinavia. Although modern shipping techniques can provide people all over the world with berries from other places, between the time delays of harvest and sorting, shipping and distributing, several days may have passed by the time a person in the United States goes to market for these berries. And although well-traveled berries remain fresh, they cannot provide a quintessential tasting experience.

When shopping for fresh berries, the main things to avoid are mold (fuzzy whiteness on the undersides of the berries) and softness. A little bit of mold is all right, but it spreads quickly. A berry is probably soft if it looks wrinkled or deflated. Moldy berries aren't good for cooking or eating. Soft berries, however, can be used for preserves or pies with no loss of flavor.

Generations of cooks have developed storage techniques that enable people to enjoy late-summer and spring berries in the middle of winter. Freezing is the most obvious method. Sealed air-tight in a rigid plastic container or wrapped snugly in plastic wrap, berries will keep up to four or five months in the freezer.

Sun-drying is a natural means of preserving the essence of a berry. In the same way that a raisin is a dehydrated form of a grape, sun-dried berries retain much of their original berry essence. Gourmet and specialty food stores carry varieties of sun-dried berries. See Sources, p. 120, for suggestions. They can be stored at room temperature, in a cupboard or in a paper bag for months and months with no loss of sweetness or flavor. For several recipes in this book—Sun-dried Berry Bagels, for example—dried berries are used to a greater advantage than their fresh equivalent. The bagels undergo a wet cooking stage followed by a dry cooking stage. Dried berries maintain their form and withstand the drastic change in cooking techniques where the fresh varieties would lose their own moisture during the wet stage and bleed during the dry stage.

Wines, juices, brandies and vinegars also capture the essence of a berry in an extremely subtle way when used reservedly. The presence of a blueberry vinegar mixed with olive oil in a salad dressing can suggest aromatically the presence of a blueberry. The same blueberry vinegar can be reduced in a pan and mounted with butter to make a creamy sauce for fish. Depending on the vehicle—olive oil or butter—and the final subject of the dish—salad or fish—you can experience the essence of blueberry in two vastly different ways.

Perhaps my favorite means of saving berries is through preserves. Preserving melts the membranes that hold a berry together, breaks down the fine fibers that keep it from simply turning into juice and, through a long and slow cooking process, transforms a bunch of whole berries into something almost completely different. It is through this process that many interactions occur. Although a recipe for preserves is a simple series of steps, it is perhaps one of the most complex chemical exchanges of berry cooking. The membranes themselves seem to dissolve in the pot and evaporate with all the steam, but they remain, helping to thicken and preserve the berries.

The uses of preserves are as diverse and plentiful as the fresh berries themselves. When added to a reduced stock, they give it body and turn it into a sauce. When added to softened butter with egg yolk and fine sugar, they make the ultimate cake frosting. When added to sour cream they make a delicately balanced salad dressing. Or they can be enjoyed simply with sweet butter spread on good bread. For me, tasting well-made preserves is like being in the center of a berry.

For the most part, each recipe in this book—as is the case with most recipes—should be viewed as a blueprint to a dish, a guideline to use as a point of reference. Many of the berries are interchangeable. The "lumpy" berries—raspberries, blackberries, loganberries, boysenberries, mulberries—are natural substitutes for one another in shape as well as taste, as are the "smooth" berries—blueberries, cranberries, currants, lingonberries, gooseberries and rosehips. These are not hard and fast categories for substitutions, just suggestions. Regional, less common berries fall into these categories as well. Try using raspberries or strawberries for cranberries and you'll become familiar with the enormous range of possibilities within the berry family. This explorative approach can be applied to other groups of ingredients as well, adding an entire new dimension to your cooking repertoire.

CHAPTER ONE · BREAKFAST AND BRUNCH

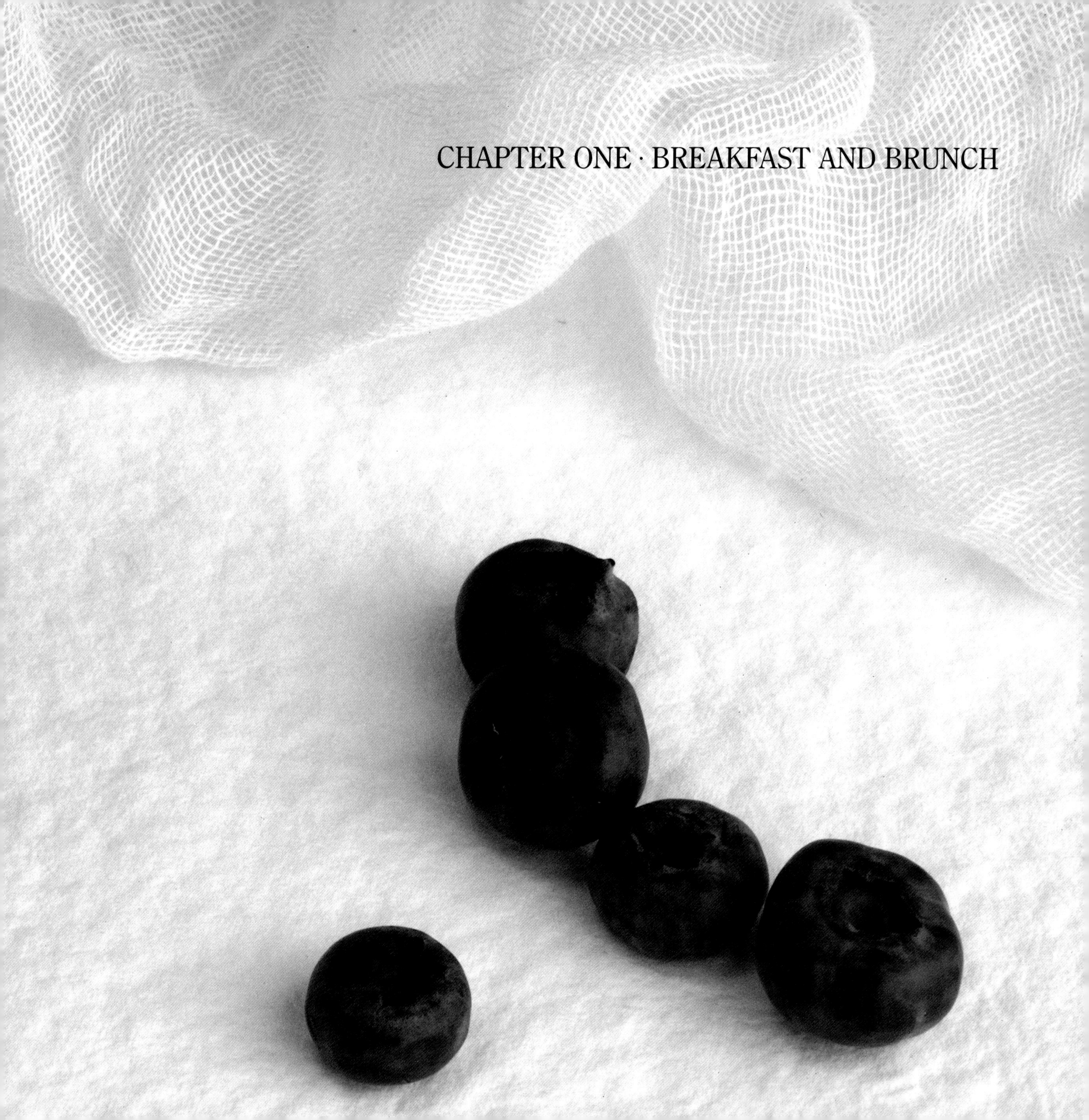

SUN-DRIED BERRY BAGELS

1 package dry active yeast
1 tablespoon sugar
1 cup warm water (about 110°F.)
4 cups high-gluten flour
1 teaspoon salt
2 eggs
2 tablespoons vegetable oil
¼ cup sun-dried blueberries
¼ cup sun-dried cranberries
2 tablespoons water
1 egg yolk

· Preheat oven to 375°F.
· In a bowl, place yeast, sugar and warm water. Let stand for 5 minutes. Yeast will foam. If the water is too hot or too cold the yeast will not foam and the process must be repeated.

· Add 1 cup of flour, salt and the 2 eggs to the mixture. Whisk together to incorporate flour.
· Gradually add the remaining flour. Incorporate it with your fingers. Continue to add flour until the dough loses its stickiness. Knead the dough for 5 minutes. This will activate the protein in the flour to make it rise, and give it elasticity.
· Coat a large bowl with half the vegetable oil. Place dough in the bowl and cover with a damp cloth. Let it rise at room temperature for about 30 minutes.
· Cut dough into 14 equal pieces and allow to rise another 20 minutes. Work the sun-dried berries into the dough pieces.

· With your finger, poke a hole in the center of each piece, and form into the shape of a bagel.
· Heat a large pot of unsalted water to boiling. Lower to a simmer. Place the bagels in the simmering water for 3–4 minutes. Turn over and simmer for another 3–4 minutes.
· Coat a large baking pan with the remaining vegetable oil.
· Beat 2 tablespoons of water with the egg yolk. Brush each bagel with the egg wash and place on the baking pan.
· Bake for about 35 minutes or until golden brown.

Makes 14 bagels.
Preparation time: 2½ hours.

BLACK CURRANT CRÊPES

2 eggs
½ cup sugar
2 tablespoons sifted, all-purpose
  flour
½ cup milk
½ cup fresh black currants
2 tablespoons unsalted butter
½ cup ricotta cheese

· In a bowl, combine eggs, ¼
  cup sugar and flour. Add the
  milk. For thinner crêpes, add
  more milk. Let sit 1 hour.
· In a 2-quart saucepan, simmer
  the black currants, just covered
  with water and ¼ cup of sugar.
  Cook for about 2 minutes.
  Remove from the water and
  let cool.

· In a 6-inch non-stick omelet
  pan, melt ½ teaspoon butter.
  When the butter begins to
  crackle, add 2 tablespoons of
  the crêpe batter, enough to
  evenly cover the pan. When it
  forms a solid coating on the
  bottom, about 1 minute, flip it.
  Continue cooking for a few
  seconds, and slide onto a large
  clean surface. Let cool. Repeat
  until all of batter is used.
· Spoon about 2 tablespoons of
  the ricotta cheese along the
  diameter of each crêpe.
· Spoon about 2 tablespoons of
  the black currants directly
  alongside the cheese. Roll each
  crêpe to form a log.

Serves 8–10.
Preparation time: 1 hour 15 minutes.

RASPBERRY PRESERVES

1 quart fresh raspberries
1 cup sugar
1 quart cold water
skins from 2 Granny Smith
    apples, tied securely in
    cheesecloth

· In a 4-quart heavy saucepan
  (copper preferred), heat all ingredients to a boil, stirring
  often.

· Reduce heat to the lowest
  possible heat and cook for 6
  hours, or until mixture is firm,
  stirring frequently. Add more
  water gradually, if necessary.
· Cool, uncovered, in refrigerator. When completely cool,
  cover with plastic or in a seal-
  tight glass jar. Can keep up to
  several months.

Makes 2–3 cups preserves.
Preparation time: 10 hours.

PECAN MUFFINS WITH MULBERRIES

½ cup pecans, finely chopped
½ cup all-purpose flour
2 tablespoons baking powder
¼ cup sugar
1 egg
2 tablespoons unsalted butter,
   melted and cooled
½ cup warm milk
1 teaspoon vanilla extract
pinch of salt
½ cup dried mulberries, or any
   dried berries

- Preheat oven to 350°F.
- Combine pecans, flour, baking powder and sugar. Add egg, butter, milk, vanilla, salt and mulberries. Let stand 10 minutes.
- Fill four cups of a non-stick muffin tray with the batter.
- Bake 8–10 minutes, or until a toothpick inserted in the center comes out clean.

Serves 4.
Preparation time: 30 minutes.

CORNMEAL MUFFINS WITH MULBERRIES AND POPPYSEEDS

½ cup yellow cornmeal
½ cup all-purpose flour
2 tablespoons baking powder
¼ cup sugar
1 egg
2 tablespoons unsalted butter,
   melted and cooled
½ cup dried mulberries, or any
   dried berries
½ cup black poppyseeds
½ cup warm milk
pinch of salt
1 teaspoon vanilla extract
zest of 1 lemon

- Preheat oven to 350°F.
- Combine cornmeal, flour, baking powder and sugar. Add egg, butter and mulberries.
- In a separate bowl, soak poppyseeds in milk for 5 minutes. Add both ingredients to the batter.
- Add salt, vanilla and lemon zest. Let stand for 10 minutes.
- Fill 4 cups of a non-stick muffin tray with the batter.
- Bake for about 8–10 minutes, or until a toothpick comes out clean when you poke it through the center.

Serves 4.
Preparation time: 30 minutes.

BLUEBERRY CORNMEAL PANCAKES

1 cup cornmeal
1 teaspoon salt
2 tablespoons honey
1 cup boiling water
1 egg
½ cup milk
2 tablespoons unsalted butter, melted
½ cup all-purpose flour
2 tablespoons baking powder
½ cup blueberries
2 tablespoons unsalted butter

· In a bowl, combine cornmeal, salt, honey and boiling water. Mix until smooth. Let cool slightly.
· Add the egg, milk and melted butter to the cornmeal mixture.
· Sift in the flour and baking powder. Add the blueberries.
· Set aside for 10 minutes.
· Melt 1 tablespoon butter in a large heavy skillet over medium-high heat.
· Pour 4 tablespoons batter into skillet for each pancake. When bubbles pop around the edges, and begin to form in the center of each pancake, flip and cook for another minute.

Serves 4.
Preparation time: 30 minutes.

BOYSENBERRY SYRUP

1 cup fresh boysenberries
1½ cups water
1 whole cinnamon stick
¼ cup molasses
¼ cup light brown sugar
1 teaspoon vanilla extract

· Place boysenberries, water and cinnamon stick in a small heavy saucepan, and cook over a low heat for about 20 minutes. Remove cinnamon stick and strain.
· Add molasses, sugar and vanilla. Let cool.

Makes 1 cup.
Preparation time: 40 minutes.

GOLDEN RASPBERRY CRUMBCAKE

1 tablespoon unsalted butter
¾ cup, plus 2 tablespoons all-
    purpose flour
1 tablespoon baking powder
½ teaspoon salt
¾ cup sugar
¼ cup unsalted butter, melted
    and cooled
2 tablespoons vanilla extract
2 eggs
2 cups golden raspberries
½ cup sour cream

CRUMB TOPPING:

¾ cup light brown sugar
½ cup unsalted butter, cut into
    small pieces
1½ cups all-purpose flour

· Preheat oven to 350°F.
· With tablespoon of butter,
  evenly coat a 7- × 9-inch
  baking pan.
· Dust with 2 tablespoons flour.
  Shake out excess. Refrigerate.
· In large bowl, combine remaining ¾ cup flour, baking
  powder, salt and sugar.
· Add the melted butter, vanilla
  and eggs. Mix until well
  combined.
· Fold in the raspberries and
  sour cream.
· Pour batter into baking pan.
  Let stand 10 minutes.
· In a separate bowl, combine
  brown sugar and butter pieces.
· Add flour and mix until evenly
  incorporated.
· Sprinkle evenly over cake batter. Bake for 30 minutes or
  until a toothpick inserted in
  the center comes out clean.

Serves 6.
Preparation time: 45 minutes.

BLUEBERRY VICHYSSOISE

5 new potatoes, washed in cold
    water
4–5 scallions, white part only
3 cups chicken stock (See below)
½ cup sour cream
1 cup blueberries
½ cup milk

· Cut washed potatoes into
  quarters.
· Cut scallions into ½-inch pieces.
· In a 1-gallon pot, heat chicken
  stock, potatoes and scallions to
  a boil. Lower to a simmer.
· Cook for about 30 minutes,
  until potatoes are soft.

· Strain potatoes, scallions and
  stock through a sieve, and
  return to pot. Bring back to a
  simmer over a low heat.
· Whisk in the sour cream. Add
  ¾ of the berries and cook on
  low heat until the first berries
  split. Set aside remaining
  berries.
· Remove from heat and chill
  overnight.
· With a fork, mash the blueberry mixture and thin with
  the milk until desired
  consistency.
· Garnish with the remainder of
  the uncooked berries.

Serves 4.
Preparation time: 1½ hours,
set overnight.

CHICKEN STOCK

2 tablespoons vegetable oil
2 large carrots, thinly sliced
8–10 shallots, finely chopped
4 scallions, finely chopped
1 Granny Smith apple, quar-
    tered with skins and seeds
¼ cup white domestic
    mushrooms, coarsely chopped
1 pound chicken wings
20–40 ice cubes, roughly 6 cups
12–15 whole black peppercorns
2–3 cloves of garlic, crushed
1 bunch parsley

· Heat oil in a 2-gallon pot.
  When the oil is hot add the
  carrots, shallots, scallions, apple and mushrooms. Cook for
  10 minutes.
· Add chicken wings, ice cubes,
  peppercorns and garlic.
· Cover all ingredients with cold
  water and top with parsley.
· Bring to a boil, and immediately lower to a simmer.
  Cook for about 2½–3 hours,
  skimming fat occasionally.
· Strain liquid, and discard vege-
  tables and wings.

· Keep chicken stock, covered,
  in refrigerator.

Makes 2–3 quarts stock.
Preparation time: 4 hours.

CRANBERRY GAZPACHO

1 cucumber
1 red pepper, cored and seeded
1 jalapeño pepper, seeded
½ green pepper, cored and
   seeded
2 tomatoes
4 scallions
1 bunch parsley
1 tablespoon lemon juice or wine
   vinegar
salt and pepper
1 cup water
½ cup fresh cranberries

· Mince cucumber, peppers, tomatoes, scallions and parsley.
  Combine in large bowl.

· Add lemon juice, salt and
  pepper. Set aside.
· In a 1-quart saucepan, bring 1
  cup of water to a boil. Cook
  cranberries for about 1 minute,
  or until a few cranberries split.
  Let the cranberries cool.
  When cool, add them to the
  gazpacho.
· Cover and refrigerate
  overnight.

Serves 4.
Preparation time: 20 minutes,
set overnight.

CHILLED RASPBERRY AND BLACKBERRY SOUP

⅓ cup red raspberries
⅓ cup blackberries
⅔ cup buttermilk
⅔ cup plain yogurt
pinch of salt

· Pass raspberries through a
  sieve and discard the seeds.
· In a separate bowl, pass blackberries through a sieve and
  discard the seeds.

· Add half the buttermilk and
  yogurt to the raspberries.
· Add half the buttermilk and
  yogurt to the blackberries.
· Add salt to each and chill 1
  hour.
· With a 4-ounce ladle pour the
  blackberry soup into a bowl,
  and a ladleful of the raspberry
  soup in the center.

Serves 2.
Preparation time: 1 hour 20
minutes.

FIDDLEHEAD SALAD WITH BLUEBERRY VINAIGRETTE

¼ cup blueberry vinegar
1 tablespoon Dijon mustard
½–¾ cup extra virgin olive oil
salt and pepper

1 pound fresh fiddlehead ferns
1 head red leaf lettuce
1 head radicchio
1 head bibb lettuce
4 bunches mâche, or lamb's
   lettuce
1 cup fresh blueberries

· In a small bowl, whisk together the vinegar and the mustard. Add the olive oil, salt and pepper.

· Drop the fiddlehead ferns into boiling water for 1 minute. Rinse under cold water.
· Wash lettuce thoroughly in clean water.
· In a salad bowl, combine the lettuce with the ferns. Toss with the vinaigrette and garnish with the fresh blueberries.

Serves 16.
Preparation time: 20 minutes.

SUN-DRIED CRANBERRY COLE SLAW

1 cup sun-dried cranberries
1 cup white zinfandel, or any
   blush wine
1 cup vinaigrette (see page 34)
1 cup sour cream
1 cup mayonnaise
1 small head red cabbage (about
   1 pound)
2 medium-sized red onions,
   sliced thinly
2–3 scallions, thinly julienned
2 tablespoons ground cumin
⅓ cup sugar
salt and pepper

· Soak cranberries in wine overnight at room temperature.

· Combine vinaigrette, sour
  cream and mayonnaise. Set
  aside.
· Remove outer leaves from cabbage. Core and cut into quarters. Slice thinly.
· Combine onion and cabbage
  with sour cream mixture. Add
  the cranberries, scallions,
  ground cumin, sugar and salt
  and pepper. Cover and refrigerate overnight.

Serves 10–12.
Preparation time: 20 minutes,
set overnight twice.

CHICKEN SALAD
WITH BLACKBERRIES

1 frying chicken, about 3½
    pounds
salt and pepper
1 cup water
1 egg yolk
1 tablespoon Dijon mustard
½ cup olive oil
2 tablespoons lemon juice or
    white wine vinegar
½ cup sour cream
1 bunch radishes, quartered
1 head chicory, broken into
    leaves
4 scallions, cut lengthwise and
    into thirds
2 cups fresh blackberries, rinsed

· Preheat oven to 400°F.
· Rub chicken with salt and
    pepper. Place chicken in a 8½-
    × 11- × 2-inch roasting pan
    with a cup of water. Roast for
    50–60 minutes. Let cool.

· Pick chicken meat by remov-
    ing skin and separating all
    meat from bones, and set
    aside.
· In a bowl, whisk together egg
    yolk and mustard. Still whisk-
    ing, gradually add olive oil and
    lemon juice or vinegar. Salt
    and pepper to taste.
· Combine the olive oil mixture
    with the sour cream. Toss
    chicken pieces with the egg-
    oil-sour cream mixture. Add
    radishes.
· Lay a bed of chicory on a
    plate. Top with ⅔ cup of
    chicken.
· Sprinkle cut scallions over
    chicken. Arrange berries on
    plate.

Serves 7.
Preparation time: 2 hours.

SHRIMP SALAD WITH RED CURRANTS

1 lemon, halved
10 black peppercorns
2 quarts cold water
12 large shrimps
4 plum tomatoes
½ cup red currants
salt and pepper
4 leaves romaine lettuce

· Place halved lemon and peppercorns in a quart of cold water. Heat to boiling; reduce heat and simmer for 5 minutes. Place the shrimp in the water and remove from heat. Let stand for 5 minutes. Drain and let the shrimp cool. Shell and devein shrimp. Discard lemon and pepper.

· In a second pot, heat to boiling second quart of water. Place tomatoes in the water and boil for about 3 minutes.
· Transfer tomatoes into ice water. Skin the tomatoes, cut in half, remove seeds and dice. Mix with currants in medium bowl. Add salt and pepper.
· Shred lettuce and arrange 2 leaves on each plate.
· Place tomato-currant mixture on top of the lettuce. Arrange the shrimp on top of the mixture.

Serves 2.
Preparation time: 30 minutes.

ENDIVE SALAD
WITH BLACKBERRIES

juice of 1 lime
2 tablespoons balsamic vinegar
2 tablespoons sherry vinegar
2 tablespoons red wine vinegar
1 egg yolk
2 tablespoons Dijon mustard
2 tablespoons honey
1 tablespoon soy sauce
1 cup peanut oil
2 tablespoons walnut oil
salt and pepper

2 heads Belgian endive
¼ cup chopped walnuts
¼ cup fresh blackberries

· Combine lime juice, vinegars, egg yolk, mustard, honey and soy sauce in a bowl. Whisk. Add oils, salt and pepper to taste. Cover and refrigerate for about 2 hours.

· Separate the outer, larger leaves of the endive and arrange on a plate. Just before serving, cut the remaining inner leaves into ¼-inch rings.
· Sprinkle walnuts and berries over the endive leaves.
· Drizzle about 2 tablespoons of the vinaigrette over salad. Refrigerate additional vinaigrette for later use.

Serves 2.
Preparation time: 2 hours, 15 minutes.

BITTER GREENS SALAD WITH STRAWBERRIES AND GOOSEBERRY VINAIGRETTE

2 tablespoons gooseberry
    preserves
2 tablespoons rice wine vinegar
1 teaspoon Dijon mustard
¼ cup safflower oil
¼ cup olive oil
2 tablespoons heavy cream
salt and pepper

10–12 small cauliflower florets
1 bunch watercress
1 bunch dandelion greens
4 ounces goat cheese
½ cup strawberries

· Whisk together preserves and
  vinegar until smooth.

· Continue whisking, while
  slowly adding Dijon mustard
  and oils.
· Add cream, salt and pepper,
  whisking gently. Refrigerate,
  covered, for 1 hour.

· Drop cauliflower into 1 cup
  boiling water and boil for 1
  minute. Remove florets from
  boiling water and run under
  cold water.
· Arrange greens on plate with
  cauliflower, goat cheese and
  strawberries. Drizzle 2 tablespoons of dressing over salad.

Serves 2.
Preparation time: 1 hour.

SMOKED TROUT AND RASPBERRY SALAD WITH LINGONBERRY DRESSING

1 cup crème fraîche
4 tablespoons lingonberry
    preserves
juice of 1 lemon
salt and pepper to taste

2 bunches arugula, washed
    thoroughly in cold water, and
    torn into bite-sized pieces
1 red onion, thinly sliced
1 whole smoked trout (about ¾
    pound), picked off the bone
    and broken into bite-sized
    pieces
8 plum tomatoes, cut into
    quarters
1 cup fresh raspberries

· In a small bowl, combine
  crème fraîche, preserves,
  lemon juice, salt and pepper.

· In medium bowl, toss arugula
  with red onion. Spread onto 4
  plates. Arrange trout pieces,
  tomato pieces and raspberries.
  Add dressing.

Serves 4.
Preparation time: 15 minutes.

FRUIT SALAD

2 medium-sized juice oranges
2 limes
¼ cup raspberries
¼ cup golden raspberries
¼ cup strawberries
¼ cup blueberries
¼ cup blackberries
1 large papaya
2 kiwi fruit, peeled and sliced
¼ cup shredded coconut

· With a sharp paring knife, remove all skin from the oranges. Holding the oranges over a medium bowl to catch juices, cut along the membranes of the oranges so the sections, or supremes, fall into the bowl as well. Repeat the process for the limes.
· Add raspberries, strawberries, blueberries and blackberries. Cover and refrigerate for 2 hours.
· Peel papaya, cut in half and remove the seeds. Cut each half into ½-inch slices and arrange on 4 plates with sliced kiwi fruit.
· Spoon berry and orange mixture, with juices, over papaya. Sprinkle with coconut.

Serves 4.
Preparation time: 15 minutes, plus 2 hours refrigeration.

CHAPTER THREE · MAIN COURSES

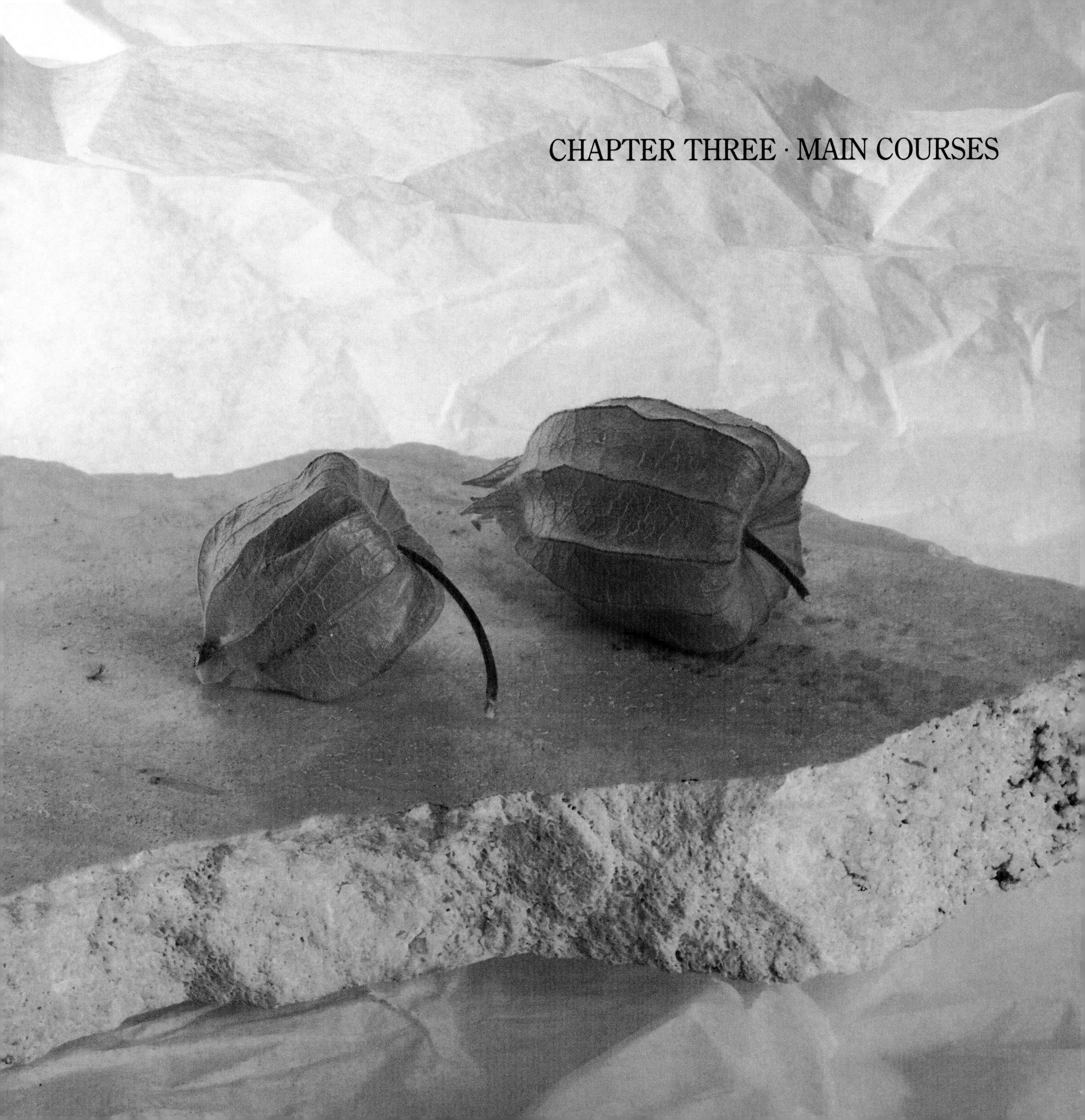

CRAB CAKES WITH BLACKBERRIES

3–4 cups boiling water
1 cup instant grits
½ cup unsalted butter
1 teaspoon salt
8 ounces Maine crabmeat, large
   lump, rinsed and cleaned
½ cup fresh blackberries
5 tablespoons sour cream
5 teaspoons black lumpfish
   caviar

· Add grits, 4 tablespoons butter
and salt to the boiling water
and stir. Lower the heat and
continue stirring. When grits
are smooth and have absorbed
all the water, set aside and let
cool.
· Combine cooked grits with
crabmeat. Add blackberries.
Form into 10 patties and chill
for 1 hour.
· In a large skillet, melt remaining butter over medium to low
heat. When butter begins to
crackle (but not burn), add the
crab cakes. Cook on each side
until golden brown.
· Serve each portion of 2 crab
cakes with 1 tablespoon of sour
cream and 1 teaspoon of caviar.

Serves 5.
Preparation time: 1½ hours.

BLACKENED TUNA
WITH STRAWBERRIES

1 tablespoon unsalted butter
5–6 large strawberries, stemmed
   and cut into thirds
½ teaspoon ground cumin
½ teaspoon ground cinnamon
½ teaspoon ground marjoram
½ teaspoon ground cayenne
   pepper
salt and pepper
2 8-ounce tuna steaks
4 tablespoons peanut oil

· In small skillet over low heat,
  melt the butter and add strawberries. Sauté strawberries for
  3 minutes, until soft. Set aside.

· Mix together cumin, cinnamon, marjoram, cayenne pepper, salt and pepper. Season
  tuna generously with mixture.
· In small cast-iron skillet, heat
  peanut oil over high heat. Sear
  fish until black, about 3–4
  minutes. Turn over, and
  blacken other side, another
  2–3 minutes. (This will produce a lot of smoke.)
· Garnish tuna with strawberries
  and serve.

Serves 2.
Preparation time: 15 minutes.

STUFFED LOBSTER WITH CRANBERRIES

2 tablespoons unsalted butter
2 tablespoons all-purpose flour
1 cup half-and-half
1 gallon plus one cup water
½ cup cranberries
¼ cup canned corn, drained, or
    fresh corn kernels
¼ red pepper, finely chopped
1 jalapeño pepper, seeded and
    finely chopped
salt and pepper
1½ pound Maine lobster

· In a skillet over medium heat, melt butter and add the flour. Whisk together for 4–5 minutes to form a roux. The roux will be extremely hot.

· Using whisk, add half-and-half slowly. Set aside.

· In a saucepan, bring 1 cup of water to a boil. Cook cranberries for about 1 minute, or until the cranberries begin to split.

· Add corn, red pepper, jalapeño and cranberries to the half-and-half mixture. Add salt and pepper. Set aside.

· In an 8-quart pot bring 1 gallon of water to a boil. Lower to a simmer. Put the lobster in the pot by holding the body, claws facing down, and cover for 6 minutes. Remove lobster and let stand until cool enough to handle.

· Split the lobster in half lengthwise with a 10- or 12-inch chef's knife. To do this, cut from the base of the head towards the tail, with shell side up. Turn lobster around and split head. With a fork, remove meat from the tail and chop coarsely. Combine with the corn-and-pepper mixture. Stuff mixture back into the tail shell. (Can be refrigerated, covered in plastic wrap, for up to 2 days.)

· Preheat oven to 425°F. Place lobster in baking dish. Bake lobster for 8–10 minutes.

Serves 2.
Preparation time: 1 hour.

GRILLED SWORDFISH WITH RED CURRANT BUTTER

½ cup water
3 tablespoons fresh red currants
¼ cup unsalted butter, softened
   to room temperature
salt and pepper
2 8-ounce pieces swordfish
1 tablespoon olive oil

· In a 1-quart saucepan, bring to
  a simmer the ½ cup water.
  Add the currants and poach
  for 1 minute. Strain currants
  and allow to cool. Combine
  currants, butter, and salt and
  pepper.

· Form the currant butter into a
  5-inch log. Place it in the
  butter wrapper, plastic wrap, or
  wax paper and refrigerate for 1
  hour.
· Preheat grill to high heat
  according to manufacturer's
  directions.
· Season swordfish with salt and
  pepper. Rub with olive oil.
  Grill both sides of swordfish
  for 3–4 minutes each, until
  tender to the touch.
· Garnish each fish with a slice
  of currant butter.

Serves 2.
Preparation time: 1 hour 15
minutes.

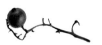

STEAMED SHRIMP
WITH CRANBERRY COULIS

¼ cup Cranberry Gazpacho
  (see page 30)
1¾ cups water
½ cup basmati rice
salt and pepper
12 medium-sized shrimp
4 tablespoons very finely
  chopped parsley

- Prepare Cranberry Gazpacho
  and set aside.
- In a small saucepan, bring to
  a boil ¾ cup water. Add the
  rice and lower the heat. Stir,
  while adding salt and pepper.
  Cover and cook for 12–15
  minutes, until all the liquid is
  absorbed. Set aside.

- In a small saucepan on medium heat, heat the Cranberry
  Gazpacho. Add 2 tablespoons
  of water and cook until the
  water is evaporated. Cover.
  Set aside.
- In a deep saucepan, bring to a
  boil 1 cup of water. Place the
  shrimp in a strainer and place
  the strainer in the saucepan.
  Cover for about 3–4 minutes,
  or until shrimp are firm and
  completely white. Set aside.
- Toss parsley with rice, and
  arrange on plate.
- Place Cranberry Gazpacho on
  the rice.
- Arrange shrimp on plate.

Serves 2.
Preparation time: 1 hour, including preparation of gazpacho.

SQUID INK FETTUCINE WITH BLACKBERRY CREAM SAUCE

1 cup boiling water
4 stalks asparagus, trimmed and
   cut in 2-inch long pieces
2 tablespoons unsalted butter
3 large shallots, peeled and
   sliced into rings
⅓ cup dry white wine
¾ cup heavy cream
3 plum tomatoes, chopped
1 cup fresh blackberries
salt and pepper to taste
2 quarts water
10 ounces fresh squid ink
   fettucine

· Blanch asparagus in boiling
   water for 1 minute. Remove
   from heat and run under cold
   water until cold throughout.
   Set aside.
· In a large skillet, melt butter
   and add shallots. Cook until
   transparent.
· Add wine and bring to a boil.
   Allow to reduce by half. Add
   the heavy cream and reduce
   mixture by half. Lower the
   heat.
· Add the tomatoes, asparagus,
   blackberries, salt and pepper.
· Heat water, lightly salted, to
   boiling in a large pot. Cook
   fettucine for 3 minutes, or
   until done. Strain and mix the
   pasta with the sauce in medium bowl.

Serves 2.
Preparation time: 15 minutes.

PAN-FRIED GROUPER WITH BLUEBERRY BUTTER SAUCE

2 8-ounce grouper fillets
salt and pepper
¼ cup flour
2 tablespoons peanut oil
⅓ cup blueberry vinegar
¼ cup heavy cream
4 tablespoons unsalted butter,
   softened

· Preheat oven to 425°F.
· Season grouper with salt and
  pepper. Dust lightly with flour.
  Set aside.
· In a large skillet, heat peanut
  oil until it smokes. Place fish
  in skillet and brown on one
  side. Turn over and remove
  from skillet. Place in baking
  pan and bake for about 6
  minutes.
· Remove fish from oven and
  return to skillet. Raise to high
  heat.
· Add vinegar and allow liquid
  to reduce almost completely.
  Add heavy cream and bring to
  a boil.
· After cream has thickened
  gradually add the butter. Add
  salt and pepper.
· Place grouper on plate and
  spoon sauce on top.

Serves 2.
Preparation time: 15 minutes.

PORK RIBS WITH RASPBERRY BARBECUE SAUCE

2 racks of pork rib (about 12
    bones each), skin peeled off
    backs
salt and pepper
1½ cups water
1 cup raspberry preserves
1 cup tomato catsup
1 medium-sized yellow onion,
    finely chopped
½ teaspoon cayenne pepper

· Preheat oven to 250°F.
· Tie the two racks together
  with non-coated string, so the
  curves of the bone face one
  another. Season with salt and
  pepper.
· Stand ribs in an 11- × 14-
× 2-inch roasting pan. Add
1½ cups of water. Cover with
aluminum foil.
· Roast for 2 hours, until your
  fingers touch through the meat
  when you pinch between two
  bones. Set aside.
· In a skillet over low heat,
  combine preserves, catsup,
  chopped onion and cayenne
  pepper. Simmer for 5 minutes.
  Add salt and pepper to taste.
  Thin with water if sauce becomes too thick.
· Cut rib racks in half, so there
  are about 5–6 bones per section. Cover with barbecue
  sauce.

Serves 4–6.
Preparation time: 3 hours.

ROAST LAMB WITH LINGONBERRY SAUCE

1 6–8 ounce loin of lamb
salt and pepper
2 cloves garlic, finely chopped
1 slice of bread, any type
¼ cup sherry, brandy or red
  wine
¼ cup chicken stock (see page
  28)
¼ cup lingonberries, fresh or in
  syrup
1 tablespoon unsalted butter

· Preheat oven to 450°F.
· Remove all fat from meat. With a sharp knife cut off the silverskin, or shiny outer skin from the meat. Season with salt and pepper. In a very hot, ovenproof skillet, briefly sear both sides of the loin, until golden brown, over high heat on stove.
· Remove from heat and rub garlic on both sides.

· Place the slice of bread in the center of the skillet and top with the lamb. This elevation helps the meat to cook evenly. Roast for 5–10 minutes, until desired doneness. The handle of the skillet will be very hot.
· Slice lamb diagonally and arrange on plate.
· Return skillet to stovetop. Over medium high heat, pour sherry into pan. Momentary flames will rise. Reduce sherry somewhat, and add chicken stock.
· Bring stock to a boil and allow to reduce for 1 minute. Add the lingonberries (drain if in syrup) and butter. Swirl pan until the butter melts evenly. Add salt and pepper to taste. Pour sauce over sliced lamb.

Serves 2.
Preparation time: 30 minutes.

BRAISED PORK CHOP WITH BLUEBERRY CREAM SAUCE

2 pork chops, 6–8 ounces each
salt and pepper
½ cup sherry
¼ cup sun-dried blueberries
½ cup heavy cream

· Preheat oven to 400°F.
· Season pork chops with salt
  and pepper.
· In a hot ovenproof skillet, sear
  both sides of pork chops over
  high heat on stove.
· Pour sherry around sides of
  skillet. Momentary flames will
  rise. When flames subside, add
  blueberries.

· Cover entire skillet with aluminum foil, and put in the oven
  for 15 minutes, until the chops
  are firm to the touch.
· Set the pork chops aside and
  return skillet to a high heat.
  Handle will be extremely hot.
· Reduce liquid by half and add
  cream. Bring to a boil and
  cook for about 2 minutes, until
  cream thickens. Add salt and
  pepper to taste.
· Pour sauce over pork chops
  and serve.

Serves 2.
Preparation time: 30 minutes.

GRILLED CHICKEN BREAST WITH GOLDEN RASPBERRY CAKES

2 cloves garlic, finely chopped
½ cup blueberry vinegar
juice of 1 lime
1½ cups virgin olive oil
1 tablespoon whole black
    peppercorns, crushed
2 whole boneless chicken
    breasts, pounded thin
1 yellow squash
1 egg
¼ cup breadcrumbs
½ cup fresh golden raspberries
salt and pepper to taste

· In a large bowl, combine the
  garlic, blueberry vinegar, lime
  juice, 1 cup olive oil and
  crushed black peppercorns.
  Place the chicken in the mari-
  nade. Let stand 1 hour.

· Grate the yellow squash into a
  large mixing bowl. Add the
  egg, breadcrumbs, golden
  raspberries, salt and pepper.
  Form 4 patties and refrigerate
  1 hour.
· Set grill to high heat according
  to manufacturer's directions.
  With skin side up, place
  chicken on the hottest part of
  the grill. Turn every 1 or 2
  minutes until done.
· In a 12-inch skillet heat remaining oil until it smokes.
  Place the cakes in the pan,
  lower heat and cook on both
  sides until golden brown.
· Serve with Rosehip
  Mayonnaise.

Serves 2.
Preparation time: 2 hours.

ROSEHIP MAYONNAISE

2 egg yolks
1 tablespoon Dijon mustard
1 tablespoon lemon juice
2 cups olive oil
salt and pepper
2 tablespoons rosehip preserves

· Combine egg yolks, mustard
  and lemon juice.
· Whisk in the olive oil drop by
  drop. Add salt and pepper.
  When mixture is firm, fold in
  preserves.

Makes 2½ cups mayonnaise.
Preparation time: 10 minutes.

CHICKEN-KUMQUAT SKEWERS WITH SPICY CRANBERRY CATSUP

10 6-inch bamboo skewers
5 whole boneless chicken breasts
20 kumquats, left whole
1¼ cups fresh cranberries
½ cup tomato paste
½ cup red wine vinegar
4 jalapeño peppers, seeded and
   finely chopped
20 shakes Tabasco sauce
¼ cup sugar
salt and pepper
¼ cup vegetable oil

- Soak bamboo skewers in water for 30 minutes to avoid burning them during cooking.
- Cut each chicken breast into 6 equal pieces.
- On each skewer alternate 3 pieces of chicken with 2 kumquats.
- Bring to a boil a large pot of water. Cook cranberries for about 2 minutes, until berries begin to split. Drain.
- Place cranberries, tomato paste, vinegar, jalapeño peppers, Tabasco sauce, sugar, salt and pepper in a food processor. Purée until smooth. Strain through a fine-mesh strainer.
- Set grill to high heat according to manufacturer's directions.
- Brush each skewer lightly with vegetable oil. Salt and pepper to taste.
- Place on the grill and cook until chicken is cooked throughout, turning often. Serve each skewer with 2 tablespoons catsup.

Makes 10 skewers.
Preparation time: 45 minutes.

ROAST DUCK BREAST WITH GOOSEBERRIES

2 tablespoons peanut oil
2 medium-sized duck breasts
¼ cup white zinfandel, or other
   blush wine
¼ cup chicken stock (see page
   28)
¼ cup gooseberries
1 tablespoon cold unsalted
   butter
salt and pepper

· Preheat oven to 450°F.
· In a heavy ovenproof skillet,
  heat oil until smoking. Place
  duck in skillet, skin side down.
  Cook for about 3 minutes over
  high heat on stove. Turn duck
  over and place skillet into the
  oven. Roast for 8 minutes,
  until firm to the touch, with
  slight resistance. Remove skillet from oven and discard
  excess oil. Slice the breasts and
  arrange on a plate. Cover and
  set aside.
· Return skillet to the stove.
  Over a high heat, add the
  wine. Raise to a boil and allow
  to reduce by about half. Add
  chicken stock and gooseberries.
  Bring to a boil and allow liquid
  to reduce. Add butter and salt
  and pepper. Pour sauce over
  sliced duck breasts.

Serves 2.
Preparation time: 25 minutes.

HOLIDAY TURKEY WITH CRANBERRY SAUCE

1 6-pound turkey
salt and pepper
1½ cups water
2 Granny Smith apples
2 sprigs fresh mint
1 stick cinnamon
3–4 whole cloves
1¼ cups cranberries
¼ cup sugar or to taste
2 tablespoons unsalted butter
2 tablespoons all-purpose flour

· Preheat oven to 375°F.
· Rinse turkey thoroughly with water. Rub evenly with salt and pepper. Open bag of giblets and rinse giblets.
· Place turkey in a 2-inch deep roasting pan with 1½ cups of water. Add giblets to water and roast for about 1½ hours or until juices run clear from the joints. Baste at 15-minute intervals. Add more water if necessary.
· Peel and core apples, reserving skins. In a cheesecloth tie skins, cores, mint, cinnamon and cloves. Place apples, cran-berries and *bouquet garni* of skins and spices in a 4-quart saucepan with enough cold water to cover ingredients.
· Cook over a moderately high heat for 1 hour. Stir often with a wooden spoon and add more water, if necessary. Lower the heat if necessary. When water is replenished, use cold water and bring back liquid to a boil; then lower to a simmer. This process will soften the apples and cranberries and make the sauce smoother.
· Remove *bouquet garni*, add sugar to taste and set aside.
· When turkey is cooked, set it aside for 10 minutes. Strain the drippings and set aside.
· To make gravy, melt the butter in a skillet and add the flour. Whisk together to form a roux. Add the drippings from the turkey pan and water, if necessary. Add salt and pepper.
· Serve turkey with gravy, warm, and cranberry sauce.

Serves 4.
Preparation time: 2 hours.

LINZER TARTS

1 cup sugar
1 cup plus 1 tablespoon unsalted
   butter
½ teaspoon salt
1 teaspoon vanilla extract
2 cups all-purpose flour
1 cup raspberry preserves
½ cup confectioners' sugar

· Mix sugar, 1 cup butter, salt
  and vanilla extract until
  smooth. Add flour. Mix until
  incorporated and dough forms
  a ball.
· Form into a log and refrigerate
  for 1 hour.
· Preheat oven to 350°F.
· Cut log into 20 equal pieces.
  Roll each piece to about ¼-
  inch thickness.
· With a 4-inch ridged cookie

cutter, press cookie shapes out
of the rolled dough. With a ½-
inch round cookie cutter, press
a hole in the center of half the
cookies.
· Butter a 14- × 17-inch cookie
  sheet with remaining butter
  and place cookies at 1-inch
  intervals. Bake 8–10 minutes,
  until cookies turn golden
  brown. Remove from cookie
  sheet and cool.
· Spread preserves on the halves
  of the cookies without center
  holes.
· Top with the cookies with
  center holes.
· Place confectioners' sugar in a
  strainer and dust over the
  cookies.

Makes 10 tarts.
Preparation time: 1½ hours.

RASPBERRY AND BLUEBERRY TARTS WITH LEMON MOUSSE

LEMON MOUSSE

zest and juice of 3 lemons
3 egg yolks
3 tablespoons sugar
½ cup heavy cream
½ cup blueberries
½ cup raspberries

TART SHELLS

1 cup all-purpose flour
½ cup cold unsalted butter, cut
  into small pieces
½ teaspoon salt
2 tablespoons sugar

LEMON MOUSSE:

· In a glass or stainless steel bowl, combine lemon zest, lemon juice, egg yolks and sugar. Place in a double boiler and stir until the mixture firms. Refrigerate for 3 hours. Mixture will continue to firm when cooled.
· While mixture is in refrigerator, prepare tart shells.

TART SHELLS:

· In a large bowl mix flour, butter, salt and sugar with fingertips.
· Add a few tablespoons of cold water to bind the dough.
· Divide the dough in quarters, and refrigerate for 2 hours.
· Preheat oven to 350°F.
· On a clean, flat surface, roll out dough and press into 4 4-inch tart pans. Bake for about 25 minutes, until golden brown. Let cool.
· While tart shells cool, remove lemon mixture from refrigerator and proceed with lemon mousse.

· In a clean bowl, whip the cream until it holds to the sides.
· Mix some of the whipped cream with the lemon mixture; then fold that mixture into the rest of the whipped cream. Spread into tart shells.
· Arrange blueberries and raspberries (¼ cup berries per tart, combined or alone) on top of the mousse.

Serves 4.
Preparation time: 3½ hours.

BLUEBERRY PIE

1 cup (2 sticks) cold unsalted
    butter, cut into small pieces
2 cups all-purpose flour
¾ cup sugar
2 teaspoons salt
4–5 tablespoons ice water
2 cups fresh blueberries
1 egg
2 tablespoons water

- Mix butter, flour, ¼ cup sugar
  and 1 teaspoon salt with fork
  or fingers until mixture has the
  consistency of coarse cornmeal. Add ice water, 1 tablespoon at a time, until dough
  binds.
- Divide the dough in half, wrap
  in plastic and refrigerate for
  about 2 hours.

- Preheat oven to 350°F.
- On a clean, dry surface, sprinkle some flour and roll out one
  of the dough patties. Press into
  an 8-inch pie pan.
- In a medium bowl, toss blueberries with ½ cup sugar and 1
  teaspoon salt. Fill pie shell
  with blueberries.
- Roll out remaining dough, and
  cut into ¾-inch wide strips.
  Arrange on top of pie in a
  criss-cross pattern. Crimp
  edges.
- Beat the egg with 2 tablespoons of water and brush
  over the surface of the pie.
- Bake for 45–50 minutes, or
  until golden brown.

Serves 6.
Preparation time: 3 hours.

BLACKBERRY CUSTARD

1 teaspoon unsalted butter
½ cup sugar
2 egg yolks
2 cups heavy cream
½ cup fresh blackberries

· Preheat oven to 350°F.
· Grease 4 6-ounce cups with
  the butter and coat with 2
  tablespoons sugar.
· Combine egg yolks and 4
  tablespoons sugar. Blend until
  mixture turns light yellow.
  Add cream. Skim off surface
  foam. Add blackberries, reserving 2 or 3 berries.

· Mash reserved berries with a
  fork. Add remaining 2 tablespoons sugar and a few drops
  of water. Set aside.
· Pour egg mixture into the
  cups. Place the cups in a 2-
  inch deep pan filled with
  enough water to reach halfway
  up the sides of the cups.
· Bake 45 minutes or until firm.
  Remove from pan and let cool,
  about 1 hour. Turn upside
  down onto a plate and cover
  with mashed berry sauce.

Serves 4.
Preparation time: 2 hours.

CHOCOLATE CAKE WITH *FRAMBOISE*-SOAKED RASPBERRIES

1½ cup fresh raspberries
½ cup *framboise*
12 ounces semi-sweet chocolate
1½ cups unsalted butter
7 tablespoons sugar
1 cup walnuts
6 eggs
2 tablespoons cornstarch,
    dissolved in 2 tablespoons of
    framboise

· Preheat oven to 350°F.
· Soak 1 cup raspberries in *framboise* for 2 hours.
· Over a double boiler combine chocolate, butter and 5 tablespoons sugar, and melt. Let cool.
· In a blender, grind walnuts into a fine powder. Transfer to a medium bowl and add eggs, raspberries and cornstarch.
· Combine walnut mixture with cooled chocolate mixture, and pour into a 12-inch springform pan.
· Bake for about 40 minutes, until firm to the touch. While cake is baking, prepare raspberry sauce.
· In a medium saucepan place remaining raspberries, 2 tablespoons sugar and 1 tablespoon of water. Over a low heat, cook for 10 minutes, stirring occasionally. Strain and cool. (Sauce can be refrigerated overnight.)
· Refrigerate cake overnight to set. Unmold and serve with sauce.

Serves 12.
Preparation time: 3 hours,
set overnight.

PISTACHIO AND ORANGE SOUFFLÉ WITH HOT BLUEBERRY SAUCE

1 tablespoon unsalted butter
2 tablespoons finely chopped
    pistachios
¼ cup, plus 3 tablespoons
    superfine sugar
½ cup fresh blueberries
2 eggs, separated
zest of 1 orange
2 teaspoons Grand Marnier, or
    other orange-flavored liqueur

· Preheat oven to 350°F.
· Butter 2 6-ounce soufflé cups.
· Combine the chopped
  pistachios with 2 tablespoons
  of sugar and dust into soufflé
  cups. Chill while continuing
  recipe.
· In a medium pan over a low
  heat, cook the blueberries with
  3 tablespoons sugar and a few
  drops of water. Add more

water if necessary. Cook until
blueberries split. Lower heat to
keep blueberries warm.
· Combine egg yolks, orange
  zest, Grand Marnier and 2
  tablespoons sugar.
· In deep, narrow bowl, beat egg
  whites until stiff peaks form.
  Fold some of the egg whites
  into the yolk mixture; then
  fold the egg yolk mixture into
  the remaining egg whites.
· Using a rubber spatula, fill the
  2 cups with the batter. Place
  the cups in a 2-inch deep pan
  filled with enough water to
  reach halfway up the sides of
  the cups. Bake 10 minutes,
  until the soufflé rises above the
  lip of the cup.
· Spoon the blueberry sauce on
  top of the soufflé and serve
  immediately.

Serves 2.
Preparation time: 25 minutes.

HAZELNUT CHEESECAKE
WITH BLACKBERRIES

1 cup blackberries
1½ cups sugar
½ cup hazelnuts
½ cup cream cheese
½ cup sour cream
½ cup ricotta cheese
2 eggs
pinch of salt
½ teaspoon vanilla extract
½ cup unsalted butter
1 cup all-purpose flour

· Preheat oven to 350°F.
· In medium bowl, combine
  blackberries with ½ cup sugar.
  Cover and refrigerate 1 hour.
· Roast hazelnuts in a shallow
  pan for 5 minutes. Cool and
  chop coarsely.

· In clean bowl, combine ½ cup
  sugar, cream cheese, sour
  cream, ricotta cheese, eggs,
  salt and vanilla. Set aside.
· In another bowl, cream ½ cup
  sugar with butter. Add flour
  and a couple of drops of water.
  Mix until the dough binds.
  Add roasted hazelnuts.
· Roll out dough and press into
  a 9-inch springform pan. Fill
  with cream cheese mixture.
· Bake for 1 hour, until the cake
  is firm to the touch.
· Chill for 2 hours.
· Cover individual slices with
  blackberries and syrup.

Serves 6.
Preparation time: 4 hours.

RASPBERRY MOUSSE

1 cup frozen raspberries,
    thawed, or fresh raspberries
2 egg yolks
2 tablespoons sugar
1 cup heavy cream
zest of 1 lime

· Strain the raspberries and
  syrup, and discard the seeds.
  Add the egg yolks and sugar to
  the raspberries.
· Place the mixture in a double
  boiler, and stir slowly with a
  rubber spatula for 10 minutes,
  until it begins to firm. Refrigerate for 1 hour. The mixture
  will become firmer as it chills.
· In a tall, narrow bowl, whip
  cream till stiff peaks form.
  Fold a bit of whipped cream
  into the raspberry mixture.
  Fold the raspberry mixture
  into the remaining whipped
  cream. Sprinkle lime zest on
  top and serve.

Serves 4.
Preparation time: 1½ hours.

COEURS À LA CRÈME

½ cup cream cheese, softened
1 teaspoon vanilla extract
2–3 tablespoons confectioners'
  sugar
½ cup heavy cream
½ cup fresh raspberries
2 tablespoons sugar

· In a medium bowl, blend
  cream cheese, vanilla and confectioners' sugar until creamy.
· In a deep, narrow bowl, whip
  heavy cream until firm.
· Mix some of the whipped
  cream with the cream cheese
  mixture; then fold the cream
  cheese mixture into the remaining whipped cream.
· Line 2 coeurs à la crème
  molds* with damp cheesecloth. Fill the lined molds with

the cream cheese mixture. Refrigerate the molds overnight
on a plate to catch whey, or
drippings.
· In a medium saucepan place
  all but 6 to 8 of the raspberries, the sugar and 1 tablespoon of water. Over a low
  heat, cook for 10 minutes. Stir
  occasionally. Add more water
  if necessary. Strain and cool.
· Unmold coeurs à la crème, and
  serve with remaining raspberries and sauce.

Serves 2.
Preparation time: 15 minutes,
set overnight.

*These molds come in two
sizes—large and small—and
are available at specialty kitchen-
ware or pottery stores.

GÉNOISE WITH LINGONBERRY BUTTER CREAM

GÉNOISE

1 teaspoon butter
1 cup all-purpose flour
6 eggs
¾ cup sugar
pinch of salt
4 tablespoons unsalted butter,
   melted and cooled

LINGONBERRY BUTTER CREAM

4 egg yolks
½ cup confectioners' sugar
1 cup unsalted butter, softened
12 ounces lingonberry preserves
½ cup heavy cream

GÉNOISE:

· Preheat oven to 350°F.
· Butter 2 9-inch round baking
  pans with ½ teaspoon butter
  each. Sprinkle each with 2
  tablespoons of flour. Discard
  excess flour. Refrigerate.
· In a bowl, whisk whole eggs
  and sugar until very firm and
  pale.
· Sift remaining flour and salt
  into egg-and-sugar mixture.
  Fold until incorporated.
· Add melted butter and continue folding.

· Pour batter into cake pans.
  Pound the pans lightly against
  a table-top to eliminate large
  air pockets. Do not bang too
  hard or the batter will deflate.
· Bake for 20–25 minutes, or
  until edges shrink away from
  the pan and a toothpick inserted in the center comes out
  clean.
· Let cool. Cut each cake in half
  horizontally.

LINGONBERRY BUTTER CREAM:

· In a bowl, blend egg yolks and
  confectioners' sugar until the
  mixture becomes a light yellow
  color.
· Add the softened butter gradually until it is evenly incorporated. Refrigerate for 1 hour.
· Add the preserves to the butter cream. Refrigerate for 1
  hour.
· In a deep, narrow bowl, whip
  the heavy cream until stiff.
· Spread the butter cream evenly
  over each cake half. Spread the
  whipped cream over all but
  one of the halves, on top of
  the butter cream. The layer
  without whipped cream will be
  the top layer. Assemble cake.

Serves 6.
Preparation time: 2½ hours.

BLUEBERRY SORBET

36 ounces lemon-lime flavored,
  carbonated soda
1 cup fresh blueberries

· Pour soda in a 2-inch deep flat
  pan. Place, uncovered, in the
  freezer. Freeze until solid.
· Remove from freezer and
  scrape frozen soda with the
  dull edge of a knife into a
  medium-sized bowl. Add blueberries to the slush.
· Cover the mixture and return
  to freezer.
· Freeze until firm.

Serves 10.
Preparation time: 3 hours.

STRAWBERRY ICE CREAM

5 egg yolks
1 quart heavy cream
1 cup sugar
1–1½ tablespoons strawberry-
  flavored liqueur
½ cup fresh strawberries

· Combine all ingredients.
· Follow instructions for your
  ice-cream machine. Use a machine with a 1½-quart capacity.
· Cover and store in freezer.

Serves 10.
Preparation time: 45 minutes.

CHOCOLATE-DIPPED STRAWBERRIES

4 ounces semi-sweet dark
    chocolate
6 strawberries

· Melt the chocolate over a double boiler.
· Holding the strawberries by
  the stem, dip each one in the
  melted chocolate until evenly
  covered. Place on wax paper
  and refrigerate.

Serves 2.
Preparation time: 20 minutes.

SUMMER PUDDING

2 cups fresh berries (raspberries,
    blackberries, strawberries and
    black currants all work well
    combined or alone)
½ cup superfine sugar
2 cups heavy cream
6 slices white bread, crusts
    trimmed off

· Toss the berries with ¼ cup of
  sugar, and set aside for 1 hour.
  Berries will give off juice.
· In a deep, narrow bowl, whip
  the cream to stiff peaks with
  the remaining ¼ cup of sugar.
  Cover and refrigerate.
· Cut the bread into 1-inch
  squares.
· In 2 goblets or small dessert
  bowls, place several berries
  along with 1 tablespoon of
  juice per serving.
· Spread 2 tablespoons of
  whipped cream on top of the
  berries.
· Cover the whipped cream with
  a layer of bread pieces. Repeat
  the procedure, layering berries
  with juice, whipped cream and
  bread pieces until the bowl is
  filled. Cover and refrigerate
  overnight.
· Top with the remaining
  whipped cream and a few
  berries as garnish.

Serves 2.
Preparation time: 1 hour, set
overnight.

CHAPTER FIVE · BEVERAGES

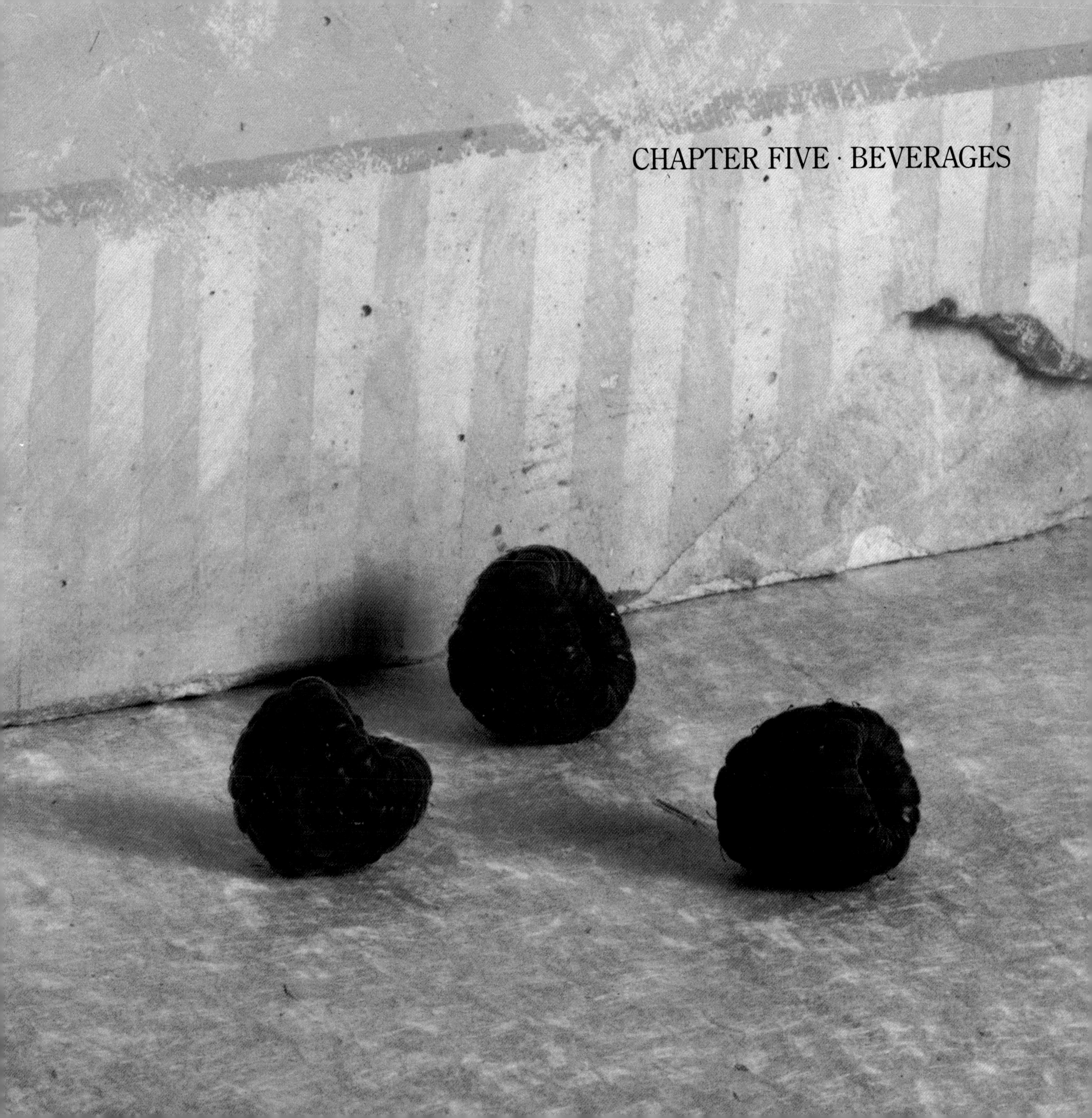

CRANBERRY GINGER TEA

2 cups boiling water
½ cup fresh ginger, thinly sliced
½ cup fresh cranberries, rinsed
pinch nutmeg
½ cup cranberry juice
2 sprigs of mint

· In a medium-sized bowl, pour
  boiling water over ginger and
  cranberries. Cover and let
  stand 20 minutes. Strain, add
  nutmeg and cranberry juice
  and stir.
· Serve warm or chilled over ice
  cubes. Garnish with mint.

Serves 2.
Preparation time: 25 minutes.

BLUEBERRY YOGURT SHAKE

2 cups plain yogurt
½ cup orange juice, freshly
  squeezed
1 cup fresh blueberries, rinsed
1 banana, very ripe

· Combine all ingredients in a
  blender. Blend on medium
  speed until smooth and frothy.
· Pour into glasses and serve.

Serves 4.
Preparation time: 3 minutes.

NUTTY RASPBERRY

¾ ounce hazelnut-flavored
   liqueur
¾ ounce raspberry-flavored
   brandy
¾ ounce heavy cream (optional)

· Combine in a cocktail glass,
   over ice.
· If using cream, combine in a
   shaker. Shake and pour into a
   glass, over ice.

Serves 2.
Preparation time: 1 minute.

FRAMBOISE
AND CHAMPAGNE

1 ounce *framboise*, or raspberry-
   flavored brandy
4 ounces champagne, chilled

· Pour brandy into champagne
   glass. Add champagne.

Serves 2.
Preparation time: 1 minute.

BERRY ICE CUBES

12 blueberries
12 raspberries

· Fill 2 ice cube trays with 1 or 2
   berries in each section. Cover
   with warm water and freeze
   overnight.

Makes 20 ice cubes, with 10-
cube trays.
Preparation time: 1 minute,
plus overnight.

STRAWBERRY MARGARITA

1½ pints fresh strawberries,
   hulled
5–6 ice cubes, crushed, roughly
   1 cup
juice of 1 lime
1½ ounces golden tequila

· In a blender, on low speed,
  combine all ingredients.

Serves 2.
Preparation time: 1 minute.

STRAWBERRY DAIQUIRI

½ pint fresh strawberries, hulled
5–6 ice cubes, crushed, roughly
   1 cup
juice of 1 lime
1½ ounces light rum

· In a blender, on low speed,
  combine all ingredients.

Serves 2.
Preparation time: 1 minute.

RASPBERRY PUNCH

1 quart ginger ale
½ cup golden rum
½ cup raspberry-flavored
  brandy
juice of 1 lime

· Combine ingredients, propor-
  tionately to taste.

Serves 10.
Preparation time: 5 minutes.

RASPBERRY EGGNOG

1 quart heavy cream
1 quart milk
4 eggs
pinch of nutmeg
2 cups raspberry-flavored
  brandy
1 cup sugar
1 quart vanilla ice cream

· Combine ingredients, propor-
  tionately to taste.

Serves 15.
Preparation time: 5 minutes.

*For both recipes, the amounts
and proportions ought to be
determined by personal taste.
Begin with all ingredients listed,
and taste as you gradually add
each ingredient.

RECIPE LIST

RECIPE LIST BY BERRY

SOURCES

The following is a list of suppliers from whom fresh berries and various berry products can be obtained. All are mail-order unless otherwise noted. It is best to call or write for individual prices, shipping costs and procedures, and availability of products.

Alaska Wild Berry Products
528 East Pioneer Avenue
Homer, AK 99603
(907) 235-8858
Jams, jellies and sauces from
   local wild berries

American Spoon Foods
P.O. Box 566
Petoskey, MI 49770
(616) 347-9030
(800) 222-5886
Preserves, jams

Balducci's
424 Avenue of the Americas
New York, NY 10011
(212) 673-2600
(800) 822-1444
In New York State
   (800) 247-2450
Fresh berries, preserves, whole
   berries in syrup, vinegars,
   sun-dried berries

Crabtree & Evelyn
Box 167
Woodstock, CT 06281
(203) 428-2766
Preserves, syrups, vinegars

Dean and Deluca
560 Broadway
New York, NY 10012
(212) 431-8369
(800) 221-7714
Fresh berries, preserves, whole
   berries in syrup, vinegars,
   sun-dried berries

Deer Mountain Berry Farm
P.O. Box 257
Granite Falls, WA 98052
(206) 691-7586
Seven varieties of homemade
   jam including gooseberry,
   loganberry and boysenberry

Peter Dent Food and Catering
120 Hudson Street
New York, NY 10013
(212) 219-0666
Berry juices, preserves, syrups

The Great Valley Mills
687 Mill Road
Telford, PA 18969
(215) 256-6648
Berries in syrup, preserves

Green Briar Jam Kitchen
6 Discovery Hill Road
East Sandwich, MA 02537
(508) 888-6870
Sun-cooked strawberry and
   blueberry jam

Harry and David
P.O. Box 712
Medford, OR 97501
(503) 776-9990
Fresh berries, preserves, jams

Kountry Kitchen
406 South Strevell
Miles City, MT 59301
(406) 232-3818
Unusual varieties of jelly including wild buffalo berry

Knott's Berry Farm
8039 Beach Boulevard
Buena Park, CA 92670
(714) 827-1776
Preserves, jams, jellies

Kozlowski Farms
5566 Gravenstein Highway
   North
Forestville, CA 95436
(707) 887-2104
(707) 887-1587
Preserves, jams, jellies

Manzanita Ranch
P. O. Box 250
Julian, CA 92036
(619) 765-0102
Preserves, vinegars, syrups

The Maury Island Farming
   Company
Box L
Vashon, WA 98070
(206) 463-9659
Fifteen varieties of jams and
   jellies, gift packs

The Silver Palate
274 Columbus Avenue
New York, NY 10023
(212) 799-6340
Berry vinegars, preserves, sauces

United Society of Shakers
Sabbathday Lake
Poland Spring, ME 04274
(207) 926-4597
Berry teas

Zambrana's/The Food
   Emporium
2346 North Clark Street
Chicago, IL 60615
(312) 935-0200
Jams, jellies, vinegars. Local
   sales only.